Contents

Leonardo da Vinci

Brandon Robshaw
and
Rochelle Scholar

Published in association with The Basic Skills Agency

Hodder & Stoughton

A MEMBER OF THE HODDER HEADLINE GROUP

Acknowledgements

Cover: Fred Van Deelin

Photos: pp. 7, 14, 17, 26 AKG, London; p. 11 The National Gallery, London/Corbis; p. 21 © HM Queen Elizabeth II, Royal Collection Enterprises.

Illustrations: Jim Eldridge

Orders: please contact Bookpoint Ltd, 39 Milton Park, Abingdon, Oxon OX14 4TD. Telephone: (44) 01235 400414, Fax: (44) 01235 400454. Lines are open from 9.00–6.00, Monday to Saturday, with a 24 hour message answering service. Email address: orders@bookpoint.co.uk

British Library Cataloguing in Publication Data
A catalogue record for this title is available from The British Library

ISBN 0 340 74267 4

First published 1999
Impression number   10 9 8 7 6 5 4 3 2 1
Year   2004 2003 2002 2001 2000 1999

Typeset by Fakenham Photosetting Ltd, Fakenham, Norfolk.
Printed in Great Britain for Hodder & Stoughton Educational, a division of Hodder Headline Plc, 338 Euston Road, London NW1 3BH by Redwood Books, Trowbridge, Wiltshire.

1 The Cave

He was fifteen years old.
He was tall and good-looking.
The sun shone on his reddish blond hair.

He stood at the entrance to a cave.
His bright blue eyes peered into the darkness.
He wanted to explore.
'Maybe there will be
something wonderful inside,' he thought.
'Something nobody has ever seen before.'

The sun beat down on his back.
Everything was still and quiet.
His home and family, down in the valley,
seemed very far away.

He stepped inside the cave.
It was dark and cool.
He went further in.
He couldn't see a thing.
He felt afraid. Should he go on?
His hands began to sweat.

What if he got lost
and couldn't find his way out again?
He had to go on.
He had to explore.
He went deeper and deeper into the cave.

Suddenly he tripped and fell.
In a panic, the boy got to his feet.
He turned and ran back towards the light.

Out in the sunshine
he threw himself down on his back.
He stared up at the sky.
A bird flew overhead.

'I want to understand everything,' he said to himself.
'I mustn't be afraid of the dark.
I want to explore every mystery.'

The boy's name was Leonardo da Vinci.
He became famous
because he did explore every mystery.
He became famous as an artist, inventor and scientist.
He lived over 500 years ago,
but the work he did
still amazes people today.

2 Childhood

Leonardo was born on 15 April 1452.
He lived in Italy, in a village called Vinci.
His name 'Leonardo da Vinci'
means 'Leonardo from Vinci'.

His mother was a peasant girl
and his father was the son of a lawyer.
They didn't get married.
Leonardo lived with his grandparents
until he was five.
Then his father married a woman of his own class.
She could not have children,
so Leonardo went to live with them.

As a child, Leonardo was bright and lively.
He was always asking questions.
He was always good at maths.
Even his teacher could not keep up with him.
He was also good at music.
He played the lyre and made up his own songs.

He was interested in everything around him.
He walked for hours in the hills on his own.
He would pick up bits of wood, flowers,
leaves, insects and draw them.

His drawings were so good
that his father showed them to an artist
in Florence.
He was called Verrocchio.

Verrocchio was very impressed.
'I would be very happy for Leonardo
to come and train as an artist with me,' he said.

At the age of 16,
Leonardo left his village.
He went to the city of Florence
to learn to be an artist.

3 Florence

Leonardo worked in Verrocchio's workshop
with some other students.
As part of his training he studied
the human body.
He had to draw lifelike figures.
Leonardo was very good at this.

His first job was to paint an angel.
Verrocchio sketched in the angel
and asked Leonardo to complete it.
Leonardo used all his skill to paint the angel.
It looked almost alive.
Its golden hair fell over its shoulders like real hair.
Its eyes were full of life.

When Verrocchio saw it he said nothing.
'Is there something wrong?' asked Leonardo.
'Oh no,' said Verrocchio, shaking his head.
'It's perfect, Leonardo. That's the problem.'

From that day on, Leonardo's teacher
never picked up a paintbrush again.
He knew he would never be as good as his student.

The angel Leonardo painted for Verrocchio.

As well as working in the workshop,
Leonardo studied on his own.
He wandered in the countryside.
He made drawings of rocks, plants and fossils.
Leonardo loved nature.
He gave up eating meat
because he loved animals so much.
He hated to see birds trapped in cages.
If he went to a market,
he would buy the caged birds
and then, in front of the stall-holder,
set the birds free.

Leonardo liked being on his own.
He made a few close friends in Florence.
but he never had a girlfriend.
Some people couldn't understand his lifestyle.
When he was 24 years old,
a letter was sent to the courts
saying that he was gay.
In Italy, in 1476, it was a crime to be gay.
The courts did not know who the letter was from.
The case did not go to court,
but Leonardo was very upset by the charge.

A year later he left the workshop.
For a while, Leonardo worked on his own.
He did some work as a sculptor.
He drew plans for inventions.
He invented a swing bridge and a cannon.
He became famous as an artist and an inventor.
But no one was paying him for the work he did.
He needed the backing of a rich man
to help him.

Then the Duke of Milan
asked Leonardo to come and play the lyre for him.
It wasn't quite what Leonardo was looking for.
But maybe in Milan
he could make a name for himself
as an artist and inventor.

In 1482, he left Florence for Milan.

4 Milan

At first Leonardo found it hard
to get work in Milan.
At that time, Italy wasn't a single country.
It was made up of lots of little city states
and it was a time of war.
People in Milan didn't trust Leonardo –
they thought he was a foreigner.

At last, some monks asked Leonardo
to paint a picture of the Virgin Mary.
He painted Mary, Jesus and the other figures.
They looked bright and full of life.
Light fell on their faces.
But the background was a strange landscape
of dark rocks.
He called the painting
'The Virgin of the Rocks'.

'The Virgin of the Rocks'.

The work took a long time to finish.
Leonardo always found it hard to finish things.
He was always getting new ideas.
The monks were angry about having to wait so long.
When they saw the painting they didn't like it.
'What's the Virgin Mary doing outside?' they asked.
'Why's she sitting on a pile of rocks?'

Leonardo looked at them and folded his arms.
He knew the painting was a masterpiece.
'I'm not changing it,' he said.

The monks took him to court.
The case dragged on for the next 20 years.

In 1495 Leonardo was asked
to do a wall painting.
It was in the dining hall of a monastery.
The painting showed the Last Supper.
Jesus ate with his disciples.
As usual,
it took Leonardo a very long time to finish.
Sometimes, he sat for half a day
just looking at his work.
A year went by and still it wasn't finished.

One of the monks complained
to the Duke of Milan.
The Duke asked Leonardo
why it was taking so long.

Leonardo said: 'I am working in my head,
even though I am not working with my hands.
I need to get a perfect idea
of what I want to do
before I do it.'

Leonardo told the Duke he'd been finding it hard
to paint the face of Judas.
Judas was the disciple who betrayed Jesus.
'But now I know what to do,' he said.
'I'll give Judas the face of that monk
who complained about me!'

The Duke thought this was funny.
He told Leonardo he wouldn't bother him again.

The painting was finished a year later.
It is one of Leonardo's great masterpieces.
It can still be seen in Milan today.

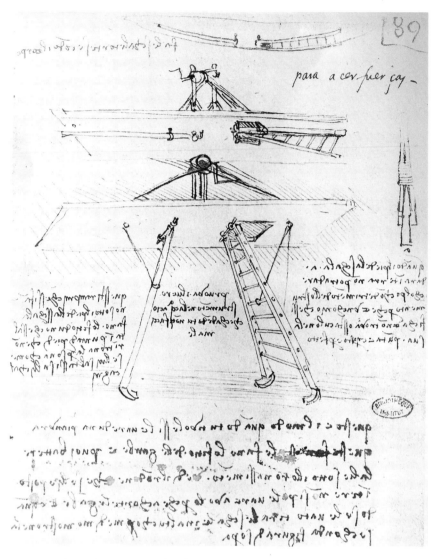

Leonardo's drawing of a flying machine.

5 'I question ...'

'I question,' wrote Leonardo in his notebooks.
Leonardo filled many notebooks with his questions.
The notebooks weren't published in his lifetime.
He wanted to keep his questions to himself.
He wrote them in mirror-writing.

Leonardo was interested in flying.
His notebooks are full of drawings
of birds' wings and flying machines.
He even made a flying machine.
In his notebook he wrote:
'The famous bird will take flight.'
One of his students said he would fly it.
The student took off from a mountain.
Leonardo watched as the machine
crashed into the ground.
The student broke his leg.

The notebooks also contain designs for
a helicopter and a hot air balloon.
Leonardo's ideas were brilliant
but ahead of their time.
500 years ago, they didn't know how
to build these machines.

Leonardo's notebooks also show plans
for propellers, submarines,
bicycles, model cities
and canal systems.
One of his best inventions
was also the simplest –
he invented metal screws.

Sometimes he worked all night in his workshop.
His friends would come round and say,
'Leave your work for a bit, Leonardo.
Come out for a drink.'

'Oh no,' Leonardo would say.
'Wine gets even with the drinker.'

Drawings from Leonardo's notebook.

Sometimes he asked his friends
into his workshop.
He showed them his joke inventions.
One day he got the stomach of a bull
and cleaned it.
He blew air into it with a pump.
As the bull's stomach got bigger,
it filled the room.
'Stop, stop, we're being pushed
into the corner!' shouted his friends.

Leonardo thought this was very funny.

Some people thought Leonardo could work magic.
But he wasn't interested in magic.
He wanted to find out scientific rules.
In his notebooks he wrote about
how sound and light travel.
'The sun does not move,'
he wrote in mirror-writing.
500 years ago, nobody knew this.
Except Leonardo.

6 The Model of the World

Leonardo stayed in Milan for 18 years.
After this he travelled around Italy.
He worked as an engineer.
He gave advice about how to defend cities.
He hated the wars,
but it gave him the chance to use his inventions.
He invented a diving suit
so that divers could attack enemy ships.

He still wanted to explore the world of nature.
He began to study the human body again.
He used to go to the hospital at night
and cut up dead bodies.
He cut up over 30 bodies.
He made many drawings of the skeleton,
the muscles and the heart.
He was the first person to draw
an unborn child in the womb.

He made friends with an old man in the hospital.
The man was nearly 100 years old.
Leonardo asked him questions about his life.
Then the old man died.

'What about that old man you made friends with?'
asked Leonardo's friends.

'I cut him up, too,' said Leonardo.
'I wanted to know why he died.'

The Pope didn't like Leonardo's study of the body.
One day, on the Pope's orders,
Leonardo wasn't allowed into the hospital.

'It won't stop me studying,' said Leonardo.
'Man is the model of the world.'

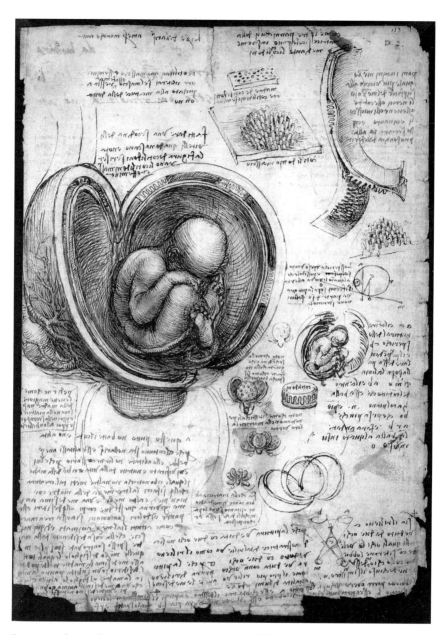

Leonardo's drawing of an unborn child.

7 Mona Lisa

In 1504, a man came to see Leonardo.
He asked him if he would paint
a picture of Mona Lisa.
Mona Lisa lived in Florence.
She was very beautiful
and Leonardo wanted her to look full of life.

Leonardo worked on the picture for two years.
When people saw it they were amazed.
They said to Leonardo, 'It's so lifelike!
Look at the way her eyes seem to follow you.
And that smile – it looks so real!'

Leonardo told the people why
she was smiling.
He had asked singers and musicians
to come and play for her
while he painted.

Leonardo never sent the picture
to the man who paid for it.
Maybe Leonardo thought it wasn't finished.
He always wanted his work to be perfect.

In 1513, Leonardo moved to Rome.
He was getting old and ill now.
But he carried on working in his workshop.
The Pope's brother paid him a salary.

Leonardo worked on inventing
a new kind of varnish for paintings.
The Pope couldn't understand the point of this.
He said, 'Oh dear, this man will never do anything.
Here he is thinking about finishing the work
before he even starts it.'

In a way, the Pope had a point.
Leonardo did have trouble finishing things.
But only because he always wanted
his work to be perfect.
Really, the Pope was missing the point.
It was because Leonardo tried to do perfect work
that his work was so special.

8 The Last Mystery

In 1516, Leonardo met the French King.
The King asked Leonardo to work for him
in France.
He gave Leonardo a house.
He visited him every day.

Leonardo was not well.
He had had a stroke.
He wanted to get his life's work in order
before he died.
His head was full of all of the things
he had not finished.

He wrote, 'I thought I was learning to live;
I was only learning to die.'
And he closed his notebook for the last time.

Leonardo as an old man.

It was 2 May 1519.
Leonardo laid his head down on the bed.
He thought back to when he was 15.
He thought back to the heat of the sun in the valley.
He thought back to the cool, dark cave
he had gone into.
His hands began to sweat.

'I want to understand everything,' he said.
'I want to explore every mystery.'

Darkness closed around him.

'Death is like another cave.
I mustn't be afraid of the dark,'
he said to himself,
as he closed his eyes.

Leonardo's Life

15 April 1452	Leonardo born in Vinci
1469	Enters workshop of Verrocchio in Florence
1472	Paints the angel in Verrocchio's 'Baptism of Christ'
1477	Leaves workshop to work on his own
1482	Moves to Milan
1483	Starts work on 'The Virgin of the Rocks'
1495–99	Paints 'The Last Supper'
1503	Failure of his flying machine
1505	Mona Lisa completed
1513	Moves to Rome and works for Pope's brother, Guiliano de Medici
1516	Moves to France and works for French King, François I
2 May 1519	Leonardo dies